THE FASCINATING
SPACE
BOOK
FOR KIDS

THE FASCINATING SPACE BOOK

FOR KIDS

500 FAR-OUT FACTS!

LISA REICHLEY

ROCKRIDGE
PRESS

Series Designer: Linda Snorina
Interior and Cover Designer: Carlos Esparza
Art Producer: Samantha Ulban
Editor: Laura Apperson
Production Manager: Jose Olivera
Production Editor: Melissa Edeburn

Photography & Illustration © Shutterstock, NASA Goddard, NASA Image Collection/Alamy, NASA,Stocktreck Images, Inc/Alamy, NASA/JPL/Space Science Institute, Science History Images/Alamy, Cover; NASA/JPL, pp. 1, 27, 60, 61, 64, 65, 70, 73, 92, 126, 129, 133, 143, 145, 149, 165; TIM BROWN/Science Source, p. 2, 97; NASA/JPL-Caltech, pp. 3, 34, 92, 98, 154, 171; PAUL D STEWART/Science Source, p. 7; NASA Goddard, pp. 9, 15, 27, 41, 73, 78, 89, 96, 158, 159, 170, 176, 203; SCIENCE PHOTO LIBRARY/ Science Source, p. 9, 76, 137, 139, 166; NASA/JPL-Caltech/R. Hurt, p. 10; NASA/NOAA, p. 14; Andrzej Wojcicki/Science Source, p. 16; NASA/SDO/ AIA, p. 20; MARK GARLICK/Science Source, pp. 21, 24, 32, 35, 88, 90; NASA/JPL/Space Science Institute, p. 28; NASA/Johns Hopkins University Applied Physics Laboratory/SouthWest Research Institute, p. 30; NASA/KSC, p. 31; NASA/Johns Hopkins University Applied Physics Laboratory/Carnegie Institute of Washington, p. 40; NASA/VRS/DETLEV VAN RAVENSWAAY/ Science Source, p. 46; NASA/JSC, pp. 48, 50, 51, 184, 190–191–192, 193; 199, NASA/JPL/MSSS, NASA/JPL/STScI, NASA/JPL-Caltech/MSSS, p. 57; NASA/JPL-Caltech/GSFC/University of Arizona, p. 58; NASA Goddard, NASA/JPL-Caltech/University of Arizona, p. 59; David Ducros/Science Source, p. 66; TUMEGGY/Science Source, p. 76; NASA/Tom Bridgman, p. 78; NASA/Aubrey Gemignani; NASA/Carla Thomas, NASA/Aubrey Gemignani, p. 80; NASA/PIA14444, p. 84; José Antonio Peñas/Science Source, p. 91; NASA, pp. 93, 109, 183, 189, 194, 195, 196, 197; NASA/H/ Richer, p. 99; Babak Tafreshi/Science Source, p. 106; NASA Goddard/ University of Arizona, p. 111; Detlev van Ravenswaay/Science Source, p. 112; NASA/JPL-Caltech, pp. 113, 114, 115, 116, 117, 118; NASA/Paul Wiegert, University of Western Ontario, Canada, p. 120; NASA Goddard/University of Arizona, p. 122; NASA/KSC, p. 123, 202; JUAN CARLOS CASADO (starryearth.com)/Science Source, p. 138; NASA/JPL/STScI, p. 142; NASA/ ARC, p. 145, 199; L. CALCADA/EUROPEAN SOUTHERN OBSERVATORY/ SCIENCE PHOTO LIBRARY, p. 146; DAVID A. HARDY, FUTURES/Science Source, p. 152, 153; NASA/CSC/JPL-Caltech/STScI, p. 160; NASA/JPL/ California Institute of Technology, p. 161; NASA/MSFC, 164, 171, 172, 188, 198; NASA/ESA/JPL/Arizona State University, p. 167. All other images used under license © Alamy, Shutterstock, and iStock.
Author photo courtesy of Tammy Snyder

Paperback ISBN: 978-1-64876-886-6 | eBook ISBN: 978-1-64876-887-3
R0

WITH MUCH LOVE TO MY HUSBAND, ZEKE, FOR SUPPORTING ME THROUGH YET ANOTHER BIG PROJECT.

Contents

Chapter 5:
Outer Space   149

Chapter 6: Space Travel — 183

Chapter 1

SOLAR SYSTEM

THE WORD **SOLAR** REFERS TO OUR SUN. WE CALL IT THE SOLAR SYSTEM BECAUSE IT'S MADE UP OF VARIOUS BODIES, ALL MOVING AROUND OUR SUN.

THE HELIO-WHAT NOW?

The prefix **HELIO** is Greek for sun. The heliosphere is the sphere surrounding the Sun over which the Sun has influence, which includes our solar system.

THE **HELIOPAUSE** IS THE OUTER EDGE OF THE HELIOSPHERE—THIS MEANS IT'S THE EDGE OF OUR SOLAR SYSTEM!

VOYAGERS 1 AND 2 are the only spacecraft to have crossed the heliopause.

The heliopause is about 123 astronomical units (AUs) or 11 billion miles from the Sun.

Earth is one AU from the Sun, which is less than 1 percent of the distance from the Sun to the edge of our solar system.

ANCIENT OBSERVATORIES

The **NABTA PLAYA** in Egypt is a stone calendar believed to align with the stars. It may be as old as 7,000 years.

Ancient astronomers from thousands of years ago tracked the movement of the stars to help them navigate, know when to plant and harvest crops, and track the seasons.

Every year on the summer solstice in June, thousands gather at **STONEHENGE** in England to see the sunrise align with the Heel Stone.

The Mayans built **EL CARACOL**, which translates to "the snail," an observatory situated high on a hill where historians believe the Mayans tracked the planet Venus.

ANCIENT ASTRONOMY

Aristotle gave us our first model of the solar system—**THE GEOCENTRIC MODEL**—which stated that the Earth stood still at the center, and the Sun, Moon, and everything else moved around it.

ARISTARCHUS OF SAMOS was the first to propose that the Sun was the center of our solar system in 270 BCE. His theory went ignored for almost two thousand years.

Astronomers once believed that all stars were the same distance from Earth and existed on a sphere called the **CELESTIAL SPHERE**.

What you may know as the **BIG DIPPER** is also known as: the Plough (UK, Ireland), the Great Wagon (Romania), Saptarishi (India), and the Saucepan (Netherlands).

In the 1500s, Copernicus correctly described the solar system as Sun-centered. This began an era of new understanding about our solar system called the **COPERNICAN REVOLUTION**.

In the early 1600s, Galileo Galilei published books that said the Sun was the center of our system. This theory contradicted the Catholic Church's beliefs at that time, and so the church forbade Galileo to teach it.

DISTANCE IN SPACE

AU stands for astronomical unit, used to communicate the distance from the Sun to the Earth, which is one AU or about 93 million miles.

Planet

1 au

499 light-seconds

Star

A **LIGHT-YEAR** IS NOT A MEASURE OF TIME; IT'S THE DISTANCE LIGHT TRAVELS IN A YEAR—ABOUT 6 TRILLION MILES.

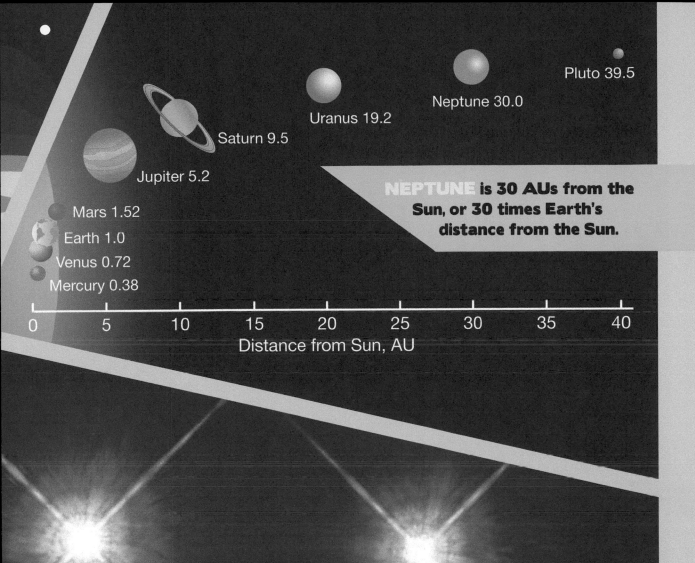

Pluto 39.5

Neptune 30.0

Uranus 19.2

Saturn 9.5

Jupiter 5.2

Mars 1.52

Earth 1.0

Venus 0.72

Mercury 0.38

NEPTUNE is 30 AUs from the Sun, or 30 times Earth's distance from the Sun.

0 5 10 15 20 25 30 35 40

Distance from Sun, AU

The next closest star system is **ALPHA CENTAURI**, a little more than four light-years away, meaning it would take more than four years to get there if you traveled at the speed of light.

WHERE ARE WE, EXACTLY?

The Sun is a **STAR**, one of 250 billion found in the Milky Way galaxy.

Any photo you see showing the entire Milky Way galaxy is an **ARTIST'S RENDITION**. We cannot take a picture of the entire galaxy.

60,000 ly

Scutum-Centaurus Arm

45,000 ly

Sagittarius Arm

Far 3kpc Arm

Galactic Bar

Norma Arm

Near 3kpc Arm

Long Bar

Outer Arm

Perseus Arm

Orion Spur

Sun

15,000 ly

Our entire solar system is a mere dot in our galaxy.

90°

30,000 ly

150°

You can see part of the **MILKY WAY** galaxy from Earth in a swath of stars across the sky, best viewed in late summer.

Our galaxy is about 100,000 light-years across, so it would take about 100,000 **YEARS** to travel from one side to the other at the speed of light.

PLANETARY PERSPECTIVE

There are eight planets in our solar system. The inner four are referred to as the **TERRESTRIAL PLANETS**. The outer four are known as the gas giants.

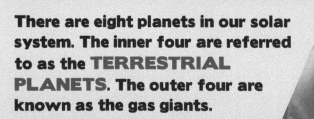

The terrestrial planets—Mercury, Venus, Earth, and Mars—are small, are made mostly of metal, and have no rings, few or no moons, long days, and short years.

The word "planet" comes from the Greek word *planetes*, which means wanderer. This name was chosen because the planets appear to wander among the stars.

THE GAS GIANTS—JUPITER, SATURN, URANUS, AND NEPTUNE—ARE LARGE, ARE MADE MOSTLY OF GAS, AND HAVE RINGS, MANY MOONS, SHORT DAYS, AND LONG YEARS.

GRAVITY'S
GOT IT

GRAVITY IS A FORCE. ALL MATTER IS ATTRACTED TO OTHER MATTER BY THE FORCE OF GRAVITY.

The Moon's gravity is one-sixth of Earth's. If you weigh 60 pounds on Earth, you'd weigh about 10 pounds on the Moon!

The larger an object's mass, the stronger the object's force of gravity.

IF **GRAVITY** CEASED TO EXIST, EVERYTHING MOVING AROUND THE SUN—THE PLANETS, MOONS, ASTEROIDS, AND EVERYTHING ELSE—WOULD FLY OFF IN A STRAIGHT LINE INTO SPACE!

The **SUN'S MASS** is more than 100 times that of all the planets and moons in our solar system combined, so its gravity is strong enough to hold all the other objects in orbit.

ORBITING PLANETS

THE EIGHT PLANETS OF OUR SOLAR SYSTEM ORBIT THE SUN ON THE SAME PLANE, CALLED THE ORBITAL PLANE.

Constellations on the orbital plane are called the **ZODIAC CONSTELLATIONS**.

Because all the planets and the Sun are on the same plane, they all take the same basic path across our sky. We call this the ECLIPTIC.

Pluto's orbit is tilted 17 degrees from the orbital plane. This is one of the reasons it doesn't quite "fit in" with the other planets.

SPACE DUST

INTERPLANETARY MEDIUM refers to the stuff that's found between the planets. Dust is just one interplanetary medium.

The solar system is a dusty place! Spacecraft have detected SPACE DUST as far out as the orbit of Uranus.

Best viewed in the middle of the night, the GEGENSCHEIN is a rare phenomenon where sunlight illuminates dust on the opposite side of the Earth.

ZODIACAL LIGHT is an illuminated cone shape that is visible because the dust on the orbital plane reflects sunlight.

Zodiacal light is sometimes called **FALSE DUSK** or **FALSE DAWN** because it occurs just before sunrise or just after sunset.

THE SUN

The Sun is almost a perfect sphere! In fact, it's the closest to a perfect sphere of anything observed in nature.

The Sun makes up 99.8 **PERCENT** of the mass in our solar system and is the only star.

Earth's atmosphere, like wearing sunglasses, makes things look a different color. For example, the Sun looks yellow to us, even though it is white.

THE **FIRST PHOTOGRAPH** OF THE SUN WAS TAKEN ON APRIL 2, 1845. THIS WAS ALSO THE FIRST PHOTOGRAPH OF SUNSPOTS.

The Sun **ROTATES**! Different latitudes rotate at different speeds. The equator rotates once every 24 days, but the poles rotate more slowly, taking 30 days.

MAGNETIC FIELDS

THE OUTER CORE OF EARTH GENERATES OUR MAGNETIC FIELD. WITHOUT THIS FIELD PROTECTING US FROM THE SOLAR WIND, LIFE ON EARTH WOULD CEASE TO EXIST.

When the **SOLAR WIND** reaches Earth's magnetic field, the particles are carried toward the poles, where they interact with gases in the upper atmosphere.

The solar wind interacts with gases to create colorful **AURORAS**. Oxygen can create red or green auroras, and nitrogen creates blue and darker red colors.

In the northern hemisphere, auroras are called **AURORA BOREALIS**, or northern lights. They are called **AURORA AUSTRALIS**, or southern lights, in the southern hemisphere.

SIZING UP
THE PLANETS

YOU COULD FIT 1,300 EARTHS INSIDE JUPITER AND 1,000 JUPITERS INSIDE THE SUN. MULTIPLYING THESE NUMBERS SHOWS THAT 1.3 MILLION EARTHS WOULD FIT INSIDE THE SUN!

Mercury is the SMALLEST PLANET. Although it's larger than Earth's moon, there are two moons in our solar system larger than Mercury: Ganymede and Titan.

Pluto is SMALL. You could fit between 150 and 155 Plutos inside Earth.

Earth is the largest inner planet and Neptune is the smallest outer planet. The outer planets are SO much larger than the inner planets that you could still fit 57 Earths inside Neptune.

All the other planets in our solar system could fit in the distance between Earth and its moon.

PLANETARY EXTREMES

URANUS HAS THE MOST DRASTIC TILT OF ALL THE PLANETS—AT 98 DEGREES, IT SPINS ON ITS SIDE!

MERCURY is named after the Roman messenger god because of its swift speed. Mercury's orbit around the sun lasts 88 days.

OLYMPUS MONS, a volcano on Mars, is the largest volcano in the solar system.

Because **SATURN'S DENSITY** is so low and it spins so fast, it has the largest equatorial "bulge" of all the planets.

VENUS is the hottest planet in our solar system because of its thick atmosphere of carbon dioxide. Temperatures there reach a scorching 880 degrees Fahrenheit (470 degrees Celsius).

Jupiter's **MASS** is so great that its gravity moves the Sun as it orbits.

NEPTUNE is the windiest planet in the solar system, with wind speed exceeding 1,200 miles per hour.

A MULTITUDE OF MOONS

There are more than **200 MOONS** in our solar system, but only three are found among the inner planets.

OUR MOON IS THE ONLY ONE WITHOUT A NAME. WE JUST CALL IT "THE MOON"!

Moons are also referred to as **NATURAL SATELLITES.**

Saturn's moon **TITAN** is the only body other than Earth in our solar system that has liquid on its surface. Titan has lakes, clouds, and rain made of methane and ethane rather than water.

Most of Uranus's moons are named after characters from Shakespeare's plays. **TITANIA** and **OBERON**, for example, are king and queen of the fairies in *A Midsummer Night's Dream*.

Some of the moons surrounding the outer planets, like Uranus's **CORDELIA** and **OPHELIA**, help their rings stay intact. These moons are referred to as shepherd moons.

Saturn currently has 82 **MOONS**, more than any other planet.

PLUTO—
PLANET OR NOT?

Pluto and its largest moon, Charon, orbit each other as a binary system. Because of this, Pluto no longer met the classification of planet and was reclassified as a **DWARF PLANET** in 2006.

The heart-shaped region on Pluto is named **TOMBAUGH REGIO** after its discoverer, Clyde Tombaugh.

The **NEW HORIZONS MISSION** was the first to visit the dwarf planet in 2015.

DWARF PLANETS

A DWARF PLANET IS AN OBJECT THAT ORBITS THE SUN AND HAS A NEARLY ROUND SHAPE, BUT HAS NOT COMPLETELY CLEARED ITS ORBIT.

Our system has five dwarf planets: Ceres (found in the asteroid belt); Pluto, Haumea, and Makemake (all found in the Kuiper Belt); and Eris (a scattered disc object; see page 34).

Originally nicknamed the Easter Bunny, **MAKEMAKE** was named after the god of fertility from the mythology of the Rapanui people of Easter Island.

HAUMEA is the first Kuiper Belt Object and dwarf planet discovered to have a ring system.

HAUMEA IS SHAPED LIKE A FOOTBALL AND IS THE FASTEST-ROTATING LARGE OBJECT IN OUR SOLAR SYSTEM, COMPLETING ONE ROTATION IN JUST FOUR HOURS.

QUAOAR is just one Kuiper Belt Object that may one day be reclassified as a dwarf planet.

SCATTERED DISC OBJECTS

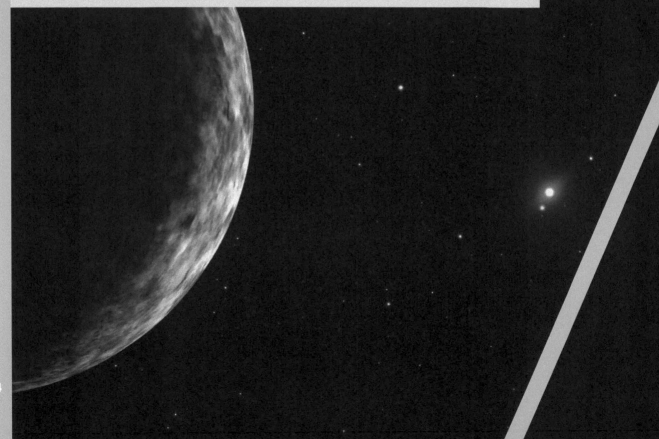

SCATTERED DISC OBJECTS (SDOs) are objects orbiting the Sun beyond the Kuiper Belt with orbits that are highly eccentric: non-circular and tilted at an angle.

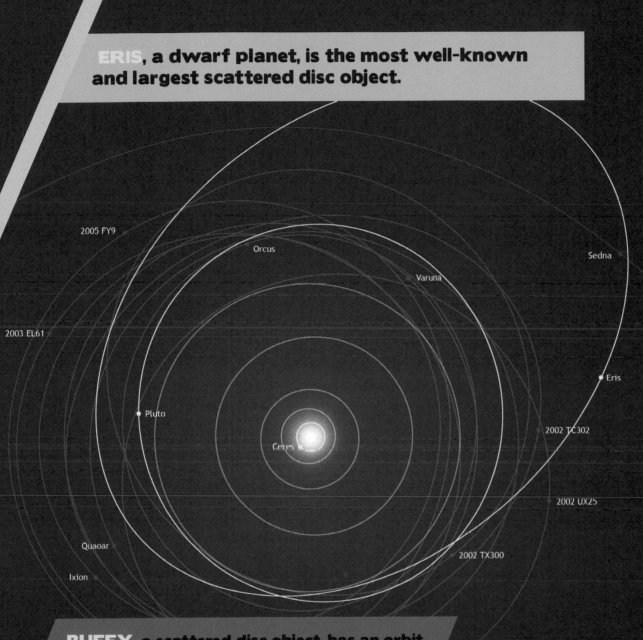

ERIS, a dwarf planet, is the most well-known and largest scattered disc object.

2005 FY9

Orcus

Sedna

Varuna

2003 EL61

Eris

Pluto

2002 TC302

Ceres

2002 UX25

Quaoar

2002 TX300

Ixion

BUFFY, a scattered disc object, has an orbit tilted 47 degrees away from the orbital plane of the rest of the solar system.

Chapter 2

PLANETS AND MOONS

OUR SOLAR SYSTEM IS HOME TO EIGHT PLANETS, FIVE DWARF PLANETS, AND MORE THAN 200 MOONS.

VIEWING THE PLANETS

When viewed from Earth, **MERCURY** is never more than 28 degrees from the Sun. It's best viewed just before sunrise or just after sunset, with the Sun just below the horizon.

AFTER THE SUN AND MOON, **VENUS** IS THE BRIGHTEST OBJECT IN OUR SKY.

Although it is not a star, **VENUS** is often referred to as the "Morning Star" or "Evening Star" because it is very bright in the morning and evening sky.

URANUS is visible with the naked eye—you just have to know where to look! In 2021, it can be seen in the constellation Aries during winter, and it will have moved to Taurus by 2023.

BINOCULARS work great for viewing the planets. You can see our Moon and the Galilean moons of Jupiter with binoculars.

TEMPERATURE EXTREMES ON
MERCURY

Mercury has the greatest temperature differential in the solar system. From day to night, the temperature drops almost 1,100 degrees!

Because Mercury lacks wind and rain, there's NO EROSION. Its cratered surface is essentially frozen in time.

It takes sunlight 3.2 minutes to reach Mercury.

During a short portion of its orbit, Mercury's orbital speed exceeds its constant rotational speed. This makes for a weird phenomenon—a DOUBLE SUNRISE!

Despite its proximity to the Sun, Mercury has ICE at the bottom of craters at its poles.

Launched in 2004, the *MESSENGER SPACECRAFT* orbited Mercury for four years, studying its surface and magnetic field.

USAF
BOEING
Sverdrup

DELTA

MESSENGER

VENUS:
EARTH'S SISTER

The clouds on Venus reflect 70 percent of the sunlight that hits them. This, coupled with the fact that it's relatively close, is why Venus appears so bright in our sky.

The Venusian **ATMOSPHERE** has more than 90 times the pressure of Earth's atmosphere.

When it rains from Venus's clouds of sulfuric acid, the liquid evaporates before hitting the surface.

VENUS IS NAMED AFTER THE ROMAN GODDESS OF LOVE AND BEAUTY BECAUSE OF ITS BRIGHTNESS IN THE NIGHT SKY.

Venus is sometimes referred to as **EARTH'S SISTER** because it's similar in size and distance from the Sun, but it cannot support human life.

Humans have landed several spacecraft on Venus; the first successful landing was *Venera 7* in 1970. Spacecraft on Venus have only minutes to transmit data to Earth before being crushed and overheated by the Venusian atmosphere.

It takes about **THREE MONTHS** for a spacecraft to travel to Venus from Earth.

EARTH IS
TEEMING WITH LIFE

EARTH is the only body in the solar system with liquid water on its surface, an ozone layer, and life.

THE **OZONE LAYER** PROTECTS US FROM ULTRAVIOLET WAVES THAT COME FROM THE SUN.

Seventy percent of Earth's surface is covered with **WATER**. A global conveyor belt of oceanic circulation helps distribute energy and nutrients throughout the world's oceans.

EARTH'S ATMOSPHERE IS 78 PERCENT NITROGEN AND 21 PERCENT OXYGEN. MORE THAN HALF OF EARTH'S OXYGEN IS PRODUCED BY ORGANISMS THAT LIVE IN THE OCEAN.

Earth is home to more than 8 million species of **LIVING ORGANISMS**.

45

THE MOON'S MARIA

WHEN GALILEO FIRST VIEWED THE MOON THROUGH A TELESCOPE, HE THOUGHT THE LARGE DARK AREAS RESEMBLED EARTH'S OCEANS. THEY ARE NOT OCEANS.

The large, flat, low areas Galileo thought were oceans are called *MARIA* (pronounced MAH-ree-ah), which is Latin for "seas."

There are 14 *maria* **on the Moon. The largest is Mare Imbrium, SEA OF SHOWERS.**

THE MOON'S CRATERS

Krater is Greek for *mixing bowl*. **CRATERS** are small bowl-shaped depressions.

THE LINE THAT SEPARATES DARK FROM LIGHT ON THE MOON IS CALLED THE TERMINATOR.

48

Craters are most visible when they fall along the **TERMINATOR**. The indirect sunlight creates elongated shadows that allow surface details to be observed.

MOON CRATERS are named after deceased scientists, mathematicians, philosophers, or explorers, including Tycho Brahe, Copernicus, Aristarchus, and Buzz Aldrin.

THE APOLLO PROGRAM

The **APOLLO PROGRAM** ran from 1961 to 1972 and executed a total of 11 spacecraft missions.

APOLLO 8 (1968) WAS THE FIRST MISSION TO ORBIT THE MOON, AND *APOLLO 11* (1969) WAS THE FIRST TO LAND ON THE MOON.

In total, 12 people have walked on the Moon. Eugene Cernan, from *Apollo 17* (1972), was the last.

The movie *Apollo 13* is based on the true story of how an oxygen tank exploded on what was meant to be the third Moon-landing mission. Instead, it became a rescue mission.

PHASES OF
THE MOON

HALF THE MOON is always lit. As the Moon orbits Earth, we see varying amounts of the lit half. This is why we have phases of the Moon.

DURING A **NEW MOON PHASE**, THE MOON IS BETWEEN EARTH AND THE SUN, SO WE CAN'T SEE ANY OF THE LIT SIDE.

The horns on a **CRESCENT MOON** are always pointing away from the Sun.

The **MOON** is out during the day just as often as it is out at night.

THE SAME SIDE OF THE MOON IS ALWAYS FACING EARTH.

During the first half of the Moon's orbit, when we see more of the lit side each night, we say the Moon is WAXING. During the second half, when we see less of the lit side each night, we say it is WANING.

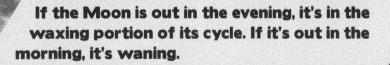

If the Moon is out in the evening, it's in the waxing portion of its cycle. If it's out in the morning, it's waning.

The Moon doesn't make any light on its own; it REFLECTS LIGHT from the Sun.

LUNAR ECLIPSES

A **LUNAR ECLIPSE** HAPPENS WHEN THE MOON PASSES INTO EARTH'S SHADOW.

Sun

A lunar eclipse doesn't happen every lunar cycle because the Moon orbits on a **FIVE-DEGREE TILT**.

On average, there are one to three lunar eclipses each year. In 1935, there were five. We won't have five in one year again until the year 2206.

Umbra

Moon

The Moon often appears **RED** during a lunar eclipse. As the Moon moves into and out of Earth's shadow, all the sunrises and sunsets on Earth are projected onto the Moon.

Penumbra

A COMPLETE LUNAR ECLIPSE CAN LAST MORE THAN ONE AND A HALF HOURS!

55

MARS:
THE RED PLANET

Mars is often called the **RED PLANET** because its surface is red as a result of iron oxide, or rust.

A year on Mars is almost twice as long as a year on Earth. Mars has a longer orbit, and it is moving at a slower speed in its orbit.

ALTHOUGH WE CAN'T FILM THERE, MARS IS OFTEN THE SETTING FOR SCIENCE FICTION MOVIES, LIKE *THE MARTIAN*.

Mars has **POLAR ICE CAPS!** They are a combination of frozen water and frozen carbon dioxide.

In 2004, NASA landed two exploration rovers on Mars: *Spirit* and *Opportunity*. The two rovers took photos and studied the surface of the red planet.

DUST STORMS are a common occurrence on Mars. But because the Martian atmosphere is so thin, their speeds top out at 60 miles per hour.

PHOBOS AND DEIMOS

PHOBOS and **DEIMOS** are small, lumpy moons found very close to the surface of Mars: just 3,700 miles and 14,573 miles away, respectively.

ASAPH HALL discovered Martian moons Phobos and Deimos in 1877.

Asaph Hall was ready to give up his search for Martian moons before he received encouragement from his wife, ANGELINE. The following night, he discovered Phobos. Six days later he discovered Deimos.

If you stood at either of Mars's poles, you wouldn't be able to see Phobos; it's too close to the surface.

PHOBOS MEANS FEAR, AND DEIMOS MEANS PANIC— UNDERSTANDABLE REACTIONS TO THE GOD OF WAR, MARS.

The largest crater on Phobos is named STICKNEY CRATER, named after Angeline Stickney Hall, Asaph Hall's wife.

Phobos and Deimos are thought to have originally been ASTEROIDS from the nearby asteroid belt that were knocked out of orbit and captured by Mars's gravity.

Phobos is slowly moving closer to Mars, and Deimos is drifting farther away.

JUPITER'S A GAS

Jupiter doesn't have a true surface area. It's a **BALL OF GAS**.

ASTRONOMERS THINK JUPITER MAY HAVE AN EARTH-SIZED SOLID CORE.

Jupiter's upper atmosphere has parallel bands of lighter clouds (called *ZONES*) and darker clouds (called *BELTS*) that move in opposite directions.

The **GREAT RED SPOT** is a storm on Jupiter that's larger than Earth. It is currently shrinking.

JUPITER'S RINGS ARE MADE OF DUST.

Despite being the largest planet, Jupiter has the **SHORTEST DAY**, completing 1 rotation in just 9 hours and 56 minutes!

GALILEAN MOONS

GALILEO discovered Jupiter's four largest moons— Io, Europa, Ganymede, and Callisto—in 1610.

Jupiter was the first planet, other than Earth, discovered to have moons. This discovery helped support the idea of a sun-centered solar system.

IO IS THE MOST VOLCANICALLY ACTIVE BODY IN THE SOLAR SYSTEM.

CALLISTO is the farthest and least active of the Galilean moons. It's also covered in craters.

SULFUR DIOXIDE enters Io's atmosphere from the volcanic eruptions. When it condenses, it turns the surface of the moon yellow!

The gravitational pull of Jupiter and its other moons has created **CRACKS** all over the surface of Europa.

The **RED COLOR** in Europa's cracks is thought to have been created by salts from a sub-surface ocean that filled the cracks and turned red from radiation.

GANYMEDE, WHICH IS LARGER THAN MERCURY, IS THE LARGEST MOON IN THE SOLAR SYSTEM.

RINGS OF SATURN

Saturn's rings contain a large amount of **REFLECTIVE ICE**. This makes it possible to view them from Earth.

THE MOST PROMINENT GAP BETWEEN RINGS IS THE **CASSINI DIVISION**, DISCOVERED BY AND NAMED AFTER FAMED ASTRONOMER JEAN-DOMINIQUE CASSINI.

Although Galileo first observed Saturn's rings, Christiaan Huygens is credited with discovering them because he was able to identify their structure.

In addition to discovering the Cassini Division, JEAN-DOMINIQUE CASSINI also discovered four of Saturn's moons.

The RINGS OF SATURN are less than a mile thick. If you happen to view them from the side, they seem to disappear!

65

CASSINI, HUYGENS,
AND THE SPACECRAFT

THE **HUYGENS PROBE** DETACHED FROM THE *CASSINI–HUYGENS* SPACECRAFT TO EXPLORE THE ATMOSPHERE OF TITAN, SATURN'S LARGEST MOON. IN 2005, IT WAS THE FIRST SPACECRAFT LANDED ON AN OUTER-SOLAR-SYSTEM BODY.

CHRISTIAAN HUYGENS discovered **TITAN**, Saturn's largest moon. He originally named it *Saturni Luna*, which is Latin for "Saturn's Moon."

Cassini studied the Saturn system for 13 years and was retired in 2017 by being intentionally crashed into Saturn.

The *Cassini–Huygens* spacecraft, nicknamed **CASSINI**, is named after Jean-Dominique Cassini and Christiaan Huygens.

THE AMAZING HERSCHELS

WILLIAM HERSCHEL discovered Uranus in 1781 with the use of a telescope he built himself.

CAROLINE HERSCHEL, William's sister, was the first paid female astronomer; she discovered numerous comets and cataloged stars, clusters, and nebulae.

The **ASTRONOMICAL SOCIETY** awarded Caroline Herschel the society's gold medal in 1828 for her contribution to the field of astronomy.

Perhaps most well-known for discovering how to make photographic images permanent, **JOHN HERSCHEL**, William's son, also made notable contributions in the fields of astronomy and chemistry.

ICE GIANTS

URANUS AND NEPTUNE ARE COLLECTIVELY REFERRED TO AS THE ICE GIANTS.

After Herschel discovered **URANUS**, astronomers realized its orbit was off. They surmised there *had* to be an eighth planet pulling Uranus farther from the Sun. This led to the discovery of **NEPTUNE**.

METHANE GAS in the upper atmospheres of Uranus and Neptune is responsible for the atmospheres' icy blue hues.

Neptune is the only planet that was discovered using **MATHEMATICAL CALCULATIONS**.

Neptune has **FIVE RINGS**, all named after astronomers who made discoveries associated with Neptune: Galle, Le Verrier, Lassell, Arago, and Adams.

Johann Galle was the first to observe Neptune with a telescope, after receiving calculations from Urbain Le Verrier, who came up with the name Neptune.

VOYAGER MISSIONS

VOYAGERS 1 AND 2 were launched in 1977. Although their primary mission was to explore Jupiter's and Saturn's systems, the missions were extended to Uranus, Neptune, and interstellar space.

Voyager 2 launched about two weeks prior to Voyager 1. The numbers were assigned according to which spacecraft would reach Jupiter first.

IN 1979, VOYAGER 1 REVEALED IMAGES OF LIGHTNING ON JUPITER!

We didn't even know Jupiter had rings until 1979, when *Voyager 1* flew past it, turned around, and took pictures of Jupiter with the Sun in the background.

In 1989, *Voyager 2* captured images of Neptune's "GREAT DARK SPOT" in its southern hemisphere. The Hubble would reveal its disappearance just five years later in 1994.

Voyager 1 took a photo of Earth at a distance of 3.7 billion miles away from the Sun. This iconic photo is called "THE PALE BLUE DOT."

Chapter 3

STARS

OF THE APPROXIMATELY 5,000 TO 6,000 STARS VISIBLE FROM EARTH, ONLY HALF ARE VISIBLE AT NIGHTTIME; THE OTHER HALF ARE BEING OUTSHINED BY THE SUN ON THE DAY SIDE OF EARTH.

SUNLIGHT, STARBRIGHT

THE SUN'S ENERGY IS CREATED BY A PROCESS CALLED NUCLEAR FUSION, IN WHICH PRESSURE IN ITS CORE FUSES HYDROGEN ATOMS INTO HELIUM ATOMS.

It's about 27 million degrees Fahrenheit in the center of the Sun. The surface is a balmy 10,000 degrees.

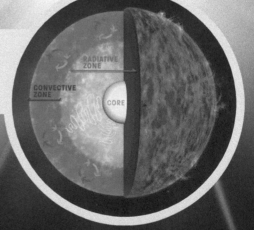

Our Sun is classified as a yellow dwarf star even though it's not actually yellow—it's white.

The light coming from the Sun is **WHITE LIGHT**. When it passes through a large amount of moisture in Earth's atmosphere, it can separate, forming a rainbow.

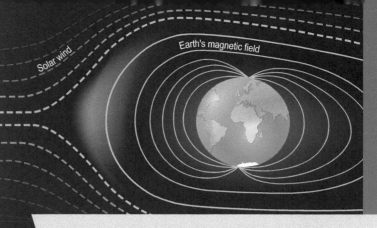

Solar wind

Earth's magnetic field

Along with light and heat, the Sun gives off charged particles called **SOLAR WIND** in all directions.

It takes sunlight 8 minutes and 20 seconds to travel from the Sun to Earth.

Earth is closest to the Sun around January 4, when it is about 91 million miles away, and it is farthest from the Sun around July 4, when it is about 94.5 million miles away.

Plants use sunlight in a process called **PHOTOSYNTHESIS** to make their own food.

SEEING SPOTS

Sunspots are visible on the surface of the Sun, called the **PHOTOSPHERE**.

A **SUNSPOT** appears as a dark spot on the Sun. The spot itself is not *actually* dark; it's just less bright than the area surrounding it.

Sunspots vary in size from 10,000 to 100,000 miles across! For comparison, the continental United States is 2,800 miles across.

Sunspots often occur in pairs and are temporary on the Sun's surface. They can last from a few days to a few weeks.

The Sun's magnetic field is about twice as strong as and 12,000 times larger than Earth's.

SCIENTISTS monitor sunspots to observe how the Sun rotates.

THE SUN'S MAGNETIC FIELD OFTEN BECOMES TWISTED AND TANGLED, PREVENTING HEAT FROM GETTING TO ITS SURFACE, MAKING IT COOLER IN SOME SPOTS. THIS IS HOW SUNSPOTS FORM.

SOLAR ECLIPSES

A **SOLAR ECLIPSE** occurs when the Moon's shadow is cast on Earth. From Earth, a full solar eclipse looks like the Sun is being blocked by the Moon.

We can only see a full solar eclipse from certain parts of Earth. The Moon is much smaller than Earth, so only a portion of Earth is in the Moon's shadow during an eclipse.

Looking directly at the Sun, even during a solar eclipse, can severely damage your eyes. When you look directly at the Sun, its light can burn the **RETINA**, the tissue in the back of your eyes.

When all but a small portion of the Sun is blocked by the Moon, it is called the **DIAMOND-RING EFFECT**.

TOTALITY is when the Moon completely blocks the Sun. It can last up to 7 minutes and 30 seconds, depending on where you are on Earth's surface.

SUN

Although the Sun is 400 times the diameter of the Moon, it's also 400 times farther away, making the two bodies appear the same size in our sky.

MOON

Total Eclipse

Umbra

Penumbra

BAILY'S BEADS look like beads of light surrounding the Moon and occur during solar eclipses when sunlight passes through the craters on the outermost edges of the Moon.

THE MOON MOVES AWAY FROM EARTH AT A RATE OF ABOUT 1.5 INCHES (3.8 CM) A YEAR, WHICH MEANS COMPLETE SOLAR ECLIPSES WILL NO LONGER EXIST IN ABOUT 600 MILLION YEARS.

TWINKLE, TWINKLE, LITTLE STAR

Optimal conditions for STARGAZING are clear skies and little to no light pollution. Allow 20 to 30 minutes for your eyes to adjust to the darkness.

Stars twinkle, but planets don't. This has to do with the way light from a distant star is scattered when it enters our atmosphere.

Stars are so far away that they look like pinpoints even when they are viewed through a telescope. If you look at a planet through a telescope, however, you will see a small disc shape.

POLLUX, the brightest star in the constellation Gemini, is 34 light-years away from Earth.

ALL THE STARS VISIBLE FROM EARTH ARE IN THE MILKY WAY GALAXY. STARS IN OTHER GALAXIES ARE TOO FAR AND TOO FAINT FOR US TO SEE.

Stars within a constellation appear to be right next to each other from our perspective. **CASTOR**, which appears next to Pollux in Gemini, is 51 light-years away from Earth.

A **SHOOTING STAR** *looks* like a star shooting across the sky, but it's not a star! It's a meteor, burning up as it passes through Earth's atmosphere.

A STAR
IS BORN

A star is born from a **NEBULA**, which is a cloud of gas and dust, in outer space.

When enough gas has collected, a nebula collapses in on itself and the pressure in the center begins the process of FUSION. Once fusion has begun, the nebula is officially a star!

THE ORION NEBULA, ALSO KNOWN AS MESSIER 42, IS FOUND JUST BENEATH ORION'S BELT. IT'S ONE OF THE BRIGHTEST NEBULAE IN THE NIGHT SKY.

SEEING STARS

Stars vary in size. We call smaller stars *DWARFS* and the largest stars *HYPERGIANTS*.

The largest known star is the **UY SCUTI**, located within the constellation Scutum. UY Scuti is estimated to be 1,700 times the width of our Sun!

The **SURFACE TEMPERATURE** of a star determines its color. Cooler stars appear red and hotter stars appear blue.

Stars come in all colors. But because of the way our eyes see color, they never appear **GREEN** or **PURPLE** to us.

Average-size stars, like our Sun, fuse hydrogen into helium for about 10 billion years, which is most of their lives. A star is most stable in this stage of its life.

Although small stars have less fuel than large stars, they also have less pressure on their core, so they burn through their fuel much more slowly and end up living longer.

DYNAMIC DWARFS

RED DWARFS are very cool, low-mass stars that live a long time—up to 10 trillion years.

About 75 percent of the stars in the Milky Way galaxy are red dwarfs.

The largest of the red dwarfs have a mass equal to about half the mass of our Sun.

Not a single red dwarf is visible from Earth with the naked eye. They simply aren't bright enough.

A BROWN DWARF is sometimes referred to as a failed star. It never gained the mass necessary to fuse hydrogen into helium in its core.

IS JUPITER A FAILED STAR? NO, IT'S NOT. JUPITER WOULD NEED TO MULTIPLY ITS MASS BY ABOUT 15 TIMES TO EVEN BE CONSIDERED ONE OF THE SMALLEST STARS.

RED GIANTS

Average-size stars expand to form what are called "**RED GIANTS**" as they run out of fuel toward the ends of their lives.

OUR SUN will run out of hydrogen and become a red giant in about 5 billion years.

When the Sun becomes a red giant, it will **EXPAND** out toward Earth's orbit, consuming Mercury and Venus in the process.

Mercury 0.4 AU

Venus 0.7 AU

The red giant phase of a star's life lasts only about 1 billion years, which is short compared with the average life of a star—10 billion years.

WHEN A RED GIANT'S CORE COLLAPSES, IT FORMS A **WHITE DWARF.** A WHITE DWARF EXISTS FOR APPROXIMATELY 14 BILLION YEARS BEFORE IT DIMS; THEN IT BECOMES A BLACK DWARF.

PLANETARY NEBULA

When a red giant dies, it leaves behind its outer layer of gas, now called a **PLANETARY NEBULA**.

A PLANETARY NEBULA CAN LAST TENS OF THOUSANDS OF YEARS BEFORE DIMINISHING.

SUPERGIANTS

Average Star

Red Giant

Stellar Nebula

Stars with a mass 3 to 50 times greater than our Sun are called **MASSIVE STARS**. They can burn through their fuel in just a few million years.

Massive Star

Red Supergiant

WHEN MASSIVE STARS EXPAND AT THE END OF THEIR LIVES, THEY DO SO ON A MASSIVE SCALE. THIS EXPANSION FORMS A RED **SUPERGIANT**, WHICH HANGS AROUND FOR LESS THAN A MILLION YEARS.

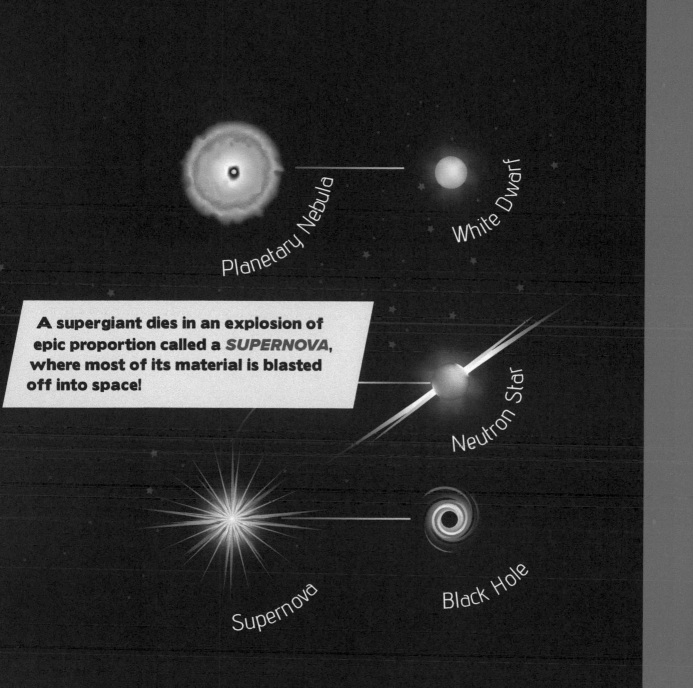

A supergiant dies in an explosion of epic proportion called a *SUPERNOVA*, where most of its material is blasted off into space!

STARS

SUPERNOVAS

In 2016, astronomers observed a supernova that occurred 4.6 billion light-years from Earth.

IT TAKES SEVERAL MONTHS FOR A SUPERNOVA TO REACH **PEAK BRIGHTNESS**. FROM THERE, IT CAN TAKE SEVERAL YEARS TO COMPLETELY DIMINISH.

If the core of a supergiant survives a supernova, it can form what's called a neutron star or, if it's massive enough, it forms a **BLACK HOLE** (more on black holes in chapter 5!).

NEUTRON STARS are extremely dense and very small—just 10 to 15 miles across.

STAR SYSTEMS

When two stars rotate around each other as a system, it's called a **BINARY STAR SYSTEM**.

Often, three or more stars will rotate around one center point of gravity. This is called a **STAR SYSTEM**.

Because we observe star systems as a single point of light in the night sky, they are given **ONE NAME** as if they were just one star.

The closest star to Earth (other than our Sun) is **ALPHA CENTAURI**. This system contains three stars: Alpha Centauri A and B, and Proxima Centauri.

The star **CASTOR**, from the constellation Gemini, is a system of six stars—three sets of binary stars all moving together.

99

ASTRONOMY
VS. ASTROLOGY

ASTRONOMY is the scientific study of the universe and everything in it. **ASTROLOGY** is the belief that the positions of objects in space affect people and events on Earth.

AQUARIUS

MARCH

TWELVE CONSTELLATIONS
BELONG TO THE ZODIAC, THE BAND OF CONSTELLATIONS THAT IS FOUND ON THE SAME PLANE AS THE EARTH, SUN, AND PLANETS.

ARIES

TAURUS

CAPRICORNUS

SAGITTARIUS

SCORPIUS

DECEMBER

LIBRA

SEPTEMBER

VIRGO

JUNE

GEMINI

CANCER

A person's **ZODIAC SIGN** is determined by which constellation of the zodiac the Sun is "in" (front of) at the time of their birth.

Zodiac signs were assigned to calendar dates 3,000 years ago; since then, Earth has wobbled. The dates used for zodiac horoscope predictions are, well, mostly wrong.

CONSTELLATION OR ASTERISM?

A CONSTELLATION is defined by boundaries in the night sky. Constellations are named after the stars found in that patch of the sky and the shapes they form.

There are 88 official constellations, including Orion, Cassiopeia, Gemini, and Leo, that make up the entire **CELESTIAL SPHERE**.

The Big Dipper is not an official constellation, but rather an **ASTERISM**—a recognizable pattern of stars. Asterisms can be part of larger constellations or contain pieces of multiple constellations.

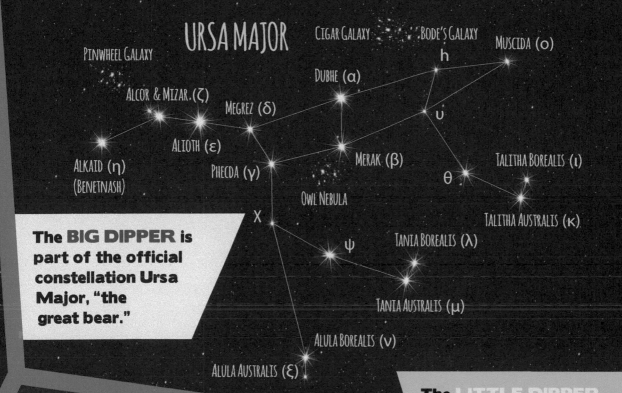

URSA MAJOR

Pinwheel Galaxy

Cigar Galaxy   Bode's Galaxy   Muscida (o)

h

Alcor & Mizar (ζ)   Dubhe (α)

Megrez (δ)

υ

Alioth (ε)

Alkaid (η)   Phecda (γ)   Merak (β)   Talitha Borealis (ι)
(Benetnash)

θ   Talitha Australis (κ)

Owl Nebula

χ

Tania Borealis (λ)

ψ

Tania Australis (μ)

Alula Borealis (ν)

Alula Australis (ξ)

The **BIG DIPPER** is part of the official constellation Ursa Major, "the great bear."

The **LITTLE DIPPER** is found in Ursa Minor, "the lesser bear."

URSA MAJOR is the third largest constellation in the sky, after Hydra and Virgo.

THE NORTH STAR

The star **POLARIS**, located at the end of the handle of the Little Dipper, is commonly called the North Star.

Ursa Minor
(Little Dipper)

Polaris
(North Star)

Ursa Major
(Big Dipper)

You can find the North Star by following the stars that make up the right-hand side of the Big Dipper.

104

The **NORTH STAR** is found almost directly above Earth's North Pole, so it stays nearly still as the other stars move around it.

Polaris is a **YELLOW SUPERGIANT** that's about 323 light-years away from Earth. Because of its distance, it's only the 50th brightest star in our sky.

ORION
THE HUNTER

Auriga

California
Nebula

Pleiades

Taurus

Aldebaran

ORION, named after the hunter from Greek mythology, is one of the most well-known and easily recognized constellations in the winter sky.

Betelgeuse

Rosette
Nebula

Orion

Barnard's
Loop

ORION CONTAINS TWO OF THE BRIGHTEST STARS IN THE NIGHT SKY: BETELGEUSE AND RIGEL.

M42

Rigel

Antares

Betelgeuse

**Betelgeuse is a RED SUPERGIANT
whose color you can see from Earth!
It is about 640 light-years away and
about 900 times wider than our Sun.**

**If Rigel were placed
in the Sun's position,
it would not quite
extend to Mercury.**

Aldebaran

Sun

Rigel

**If Betelgeuse took the place
of our Sun, its surface would
extend beyond the orbit of
Jupiter!**

**Rigel is a BLUE-WHITE
SUPERGIANT and appears
blue in our sky. It is about 870
light-years away and 79 times
wider than our Sun.**

**In Greek mythology, Orion fell in love with the PLEIADES, also
called the Seven Sisters. The Pleiades were placed in the sky on the
other side of Taurus, where Orion continues to pursue them.**

107

CANIS MAJOR

MULIPHEIN

SIRIUS

MIRZAM

Canis Major's brightest star, **SIRIUS**, can be found by following the imaginary line created from the three stars in Orion's belt to the constellation's lower left.

CANIS MAJOR, THE DOG CONSTELLATION, IS VISIBLE IN THE NORTHERN HEMISPHERE FROM JANUARY THROUGH MARCH, IN THE SOUTHERN SKY.

WEZEN

ADHARA

FURUD

ALUDRA

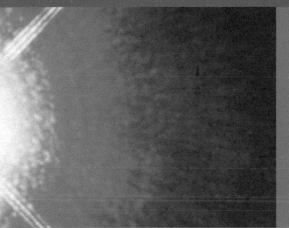

Sirius is just 8.6 light-years away from Earth and is a **BINARY SYSTEM**. The larger star is Sirius A and the smaller is Sirius B.

The brighter of the two stars, **SIRIUS A**, is more than 25 times brighter than our Sun. Because it's also relatively close to us, it is the brightest star in our night sky!

Canis Major is Latin for "the great dog." The smaller dog, **CANIS MINOR**, is found just next to Canis Major and to the left of Orion.

Canis Major is often depicted as pursuing the hare of the constellation **LEPUS**, directly beneath Orion.

109

Chapter 4
ASTEROIDS, COMETS, AND METEORS

METEORS, ALSO CALLED SHOOTING STARS, OCCUR WHEN A PIECE OF AN ASTEROID OR COMET ENTERS EARTH'S ATMOSPHERE AND CREATES A STREAK OF LIGHT ACROSS THE SKY AS IT BURNS UP.

THE ASTEROID BELT

The Asteroid Belt is also called the **MAIN BELT** because although asteroids are found in other places in our solar system, most are found in this "main" region.

IN MOVIES, SPACESHIPS OFTEN DUCK AND WEAVE TO AVOID IMPACT IN THE ASTEROID BELT. THIS IS INACCURATE. THE AVERAGE DISTANCE BETWEEN ASTEROIDS IS MORE THAN HALF A MILLION MILES.

The asteroid belt is found between the orbits of Mars and Jupiter, between 2.2 and 3.2 AU from the Sun, and contains **MILLIONS OF ASTEROIDS**.

ASTEROIDS ARE MADE OF ROCK AND METAL. THEY CAN BE AS SMALL AS A PEBBLE OR AS BIG AS 300 MILES ACROSS.

Asteroids found in the orbit of a planet are called TROJANS. Of all the planets in our solar system, Jupiter has the most trojans—more than 9,800!

Earth has one trojan, named 2010 TK7. It will never collide with Earth. Trojans are locked in a position where they stay either just ahead or just behind a planet.

In October 2021, the *Lucy* spacecraft will launch NASA's first ever mission to explore the JUPITER TROJANS. It will take 12 years for *Lucy* to get there.

CERES

THE **SMALLEST** OF THE DWARF PLANETS, CERES IS THE ONLY ONE IN THE ASTEROID BELT — THE OTHERS ARE FOUND BEYOND NEPTUNE.

CERES was the first object discovered in the asteroid belt. Prior to its discovery, we didn't even know the asteroid belt existed!

CERES IS THE ONLY **DWARF PLANET**, AND THE LARGEST OBJECT, FOUND IN THE ASTEROID BELT — IT MAKES UP 25 PERCENT OF THE MASS OF THE ASTEROID BELT.

Ceres was discovered in 1801 by Italian astronomer **GIUSEPPE PIAZZI**. It was first believed to be a comet, then a planet, then an asteroid, and was finally named a dwarf planet in 2006.

The spacecraft *Dawn* visited Ceres in 2015, making it the first dwarf planet visited by spacecraft.

AN OCEAN BENEATH THE CRUST OF CERES HAS FILLED ITS CRATERS WITH SALT. THIS MAKES ITS CRATERS REFLECTIVE.

In 2006, when Pluto was demoted to the status of dwarf planet, Ceres was *upgraded* to the status of dwarf planet.

Pluto   Eris   Haumea   Makemake   Ceres

VESTA

VESTA is an asteroid and is the second largest object in the main asteroid belt, after Ceres. Although Ceres was upgraded to dwarf planet, Vesta was not.

You can sometimes see Vesta, the **BRIGHTEST** object in the asteroid belt, with the naked eye.

Up to 6 percent of **METEORITES** found on Earth are believed to be pieces of Vesta.

Vesta has a crust, a mantle, and a core, just like Earth. Astronomers think it was a **PROTOPLANET**, or the beginning of a planet, that never fully formed.

VESTA'S RHEASILVIA BASIN

Vesta was involved in a collision that created a large crater at its south pole, the **RHEASILVIA BASIN**, which is 95 percent of its total diameter.

The Rheasilvia Basin is 12 miles deep, which is about 12 times deeper than the **GRAND CANYON**.

Vesta is home to the solar system's second-largest mountain, the RHEASILVIA BASIN CENTRAL PEAK. At about 14 miles (22.5 km) high, it's more than twice as high as Mount Everest (5.5 miles, or 8.9 km, tall).

NEAR-EARTH OBJECTS

NEO, or near-Earth objects, are comets and asteroids orbiting the Sun near Earth.

If an asteroid enters our atmosphere, we call it a meteor, which can also be called a SHOOTING STAR.

NASA runs the NEO Observations Program, which monitors and tracks NEOs. So far, the program has identified more than 25,000 NEOs!

DESTINATION: BENNU

BENNU is a **NEO** that orbits the Sun at an average distance of 105 million miles, putting it just beyond Earth's orbit.

Bennu is a pile of rubble held together by **GRAVITY**. In fact, Bennu may be 20 to 40 percent air pockets.

Bennu was named after the Egyptian mythological **BIRD** that resembles a heron, as part of a 2012 naming contest held by **NASA**.

In 2016, NASA launched the OSIRIS-REx mission to collect samples from NEO Bennu. NASA confirmed that it had collected samples in 2020 and that it will return to Earth in 2023.

Bennu was chosen for the OSIRIS-REx mission because it has a diameter of 500 meters, orbits close to Earth, and is carbon-rich.

ASTEROID ODDITIES

In 2013, scientists discovered that an asteroid named **CHARIKLO** has rings! The asteroid itself is only 188 miles wide.

In 1993, the asteroid Ida was discovered to have a moon, **DACTYL**. This led to the discovery that one-sixth of asteroids have at least one moon.

In 2005, **ITOKAWA** became the first asteroid on which humans were able to successfully land a spacecraft, collect samples, and return them to Earth.

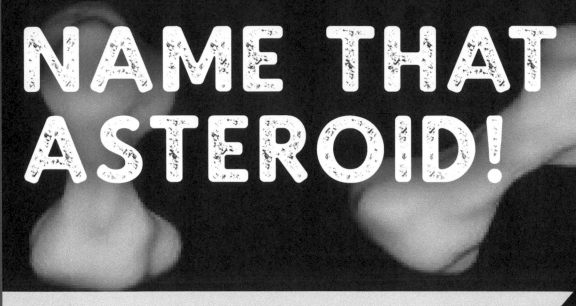

NAME THAT ASTEROID!

KLEOPATRA, a dog bone–shaped asteroid in the main belt, is named after the Egyptian queen. Its moons, Cleoselene and **ALEXHELIOS**, are named after Cleopatra's twins.

Asteroid 564 is named **DUDU**, after a character in Friedrich Nietzsche's *Thus Spoke Zarathustra.*

Asteroid 12410 in the asteroid belt is named **DONALD DUCK**, after the Disney cartoon character.

In 1985, astronomer James Gibson named asteroid 2309 after his cat, **MR. SPOCK**. The cat was named after the *Star Trek* character.

Asteroids 4147 to 4150 are named Lennon, McCartney, Harrison, and Starr, after members of **THE BEATLES**.

127

FIRE IN THE SKY

ON AN AVERAGE NIGHT WITH GOOD VISIBILITY, YOU CAN OBSERVE TWO TO THREE SHOOTING STARS PER HOUR.

A shooting star that is larger and brighter than usual is called a FIREBALL.

Fireballs are created by METEORS that are wider than one meter. A meteor of this size enters Earth's atmosphere about 40 times per year.

ON JUNE 30, 1908, A FIREBALL EXPLODED OVER **SIBERIA**, FLATTENING 80 MILLION TREES.

INTERNATIONAL ASTEROID DAY JUNE 30

June 30 is now recognized as **INTERNATIONAL ASTEROID DAY**. Held on the day of the Siberia fireball event, it aims to raise awareness of the threat of NEOs colliding with Earth.

MOST FIREBALLS EXPLODE INTO SMALLER PIECES BEFORE MAKING IT TO EARTH'S SURFACE. THIS EXPLOSION IS CAUSED BY **FRICTION** BETWEEN THE METEOR AND EARTH'S ATMOSPHERE.

In February 2013, a fireball exploded over Russia. The asteroid was about 56 feet (17 m) long and weighed 11,000 tons. There were no deaths, but more than 1,100 people were injured.

Some observers report hearing sounds associated with fireballs exploding, from **SONIC BOOMS** to **FIZZING** noises.

METEOR SHOWERS

METEOR SHOWERS occur when Earth passes through regions of its orbit that contain debris, most commonly left behind by comets.

Even though meteor showers are named after a **CONSTELLATION**, they are not actually coming *from* the constellation they were named for.

The Perseid meteor shower occurs in early to mid-August every year. The meteors in Perseid appear to radiate from the constellation PERSEUS.

THE PERSEID METEOR SHOWER IS CREATED FROM BITS OF THE SWIFT-TUTTLE COMET. SWIFT-TUTTLE WAS LAST VISIBLE FROM EARTH IN 1992 AND HAS AN ORBIT AROUND THE SUN OF 133 YEARS.

METEORITES

If any piece of a **METEOR** survives the journey through our atmosphere to the surface of Earth, it becomes a **METEORITE**.

EVERY SQUARE MILE ON EARTH CAN EXPECT, ON AVERAGE, ONE METEORITE TO LAND ON IT ONCE EVERY 20,000 YEARS!

The largest meteorite to land on Earth (that we know of) is the **HOBA METEORITE**. It landed in Namibia in 1920 and weighed 60 tons.

METEORITES ARE COATED IN A BLACK CRUST ON THEIR SURFACE, ARE VERY DENSE, HAVE SMOOTH DENTS AND EDGES, AND ARE OFTEN MAGNETIC.

In 1992, a bowling ball–sized meteorite landed on a parked car (a 1980 Chevrolet Malibu) in Peekskill, New York. It is now known as the **PEEKSKILL METEORITE**.

In November 2020, a 4.5-pound meteorite crashed through the awning of a home in **INDONESIA**. It was sold for almost 2 million dollars!

PHAËTHON AND THE GEMINID METEOR SHOWERS

PHAËTHON is an asteroid that passes close to the Sun, like a comet, then flies out past the orbit of Mars and comes back.

When closest to the sun, Phaëthon's temperature reaches 1,500 degrees Fahrenheit, which makes the metal on its surface both **TACKY** and **BLUE**.

The Geminid meteor shower is created by debris from **PHAËTHON**. It's the only meteor shower created by something other than a comet.

The **GEMINID METEOR SHOWER** peaks each year in mid-December. In perfect conditions, you can see up to 120 meteors per hour—that's a shooting star every 30 seconds!

COMETS, COMETS, COMETS

The word *COMET* comes from the Greek word *kometes*, which translates as **"LONG-HAIRED STAR."**

A comet is a sometimes called a **"DIRTY SNOWBALL"** because it's a ball of ice with dust and rock mixed in.

Most comets have **TWO TAILS**. The first is created by a trail of dust showing the path it took, and the second is ice being blasted from the comet's surface—this tail is always pointed away from the Sun.

The **SPEED** of a comet varies in its orbit. Its fastest speed as it gets whipped around the Sun can be up to 100,000 miles per hour.

Each time a comet travels around the Sun, it loses mass as the ice vaporizes to form one tail and the loosened dust forms the other.

The **TAIL OF A COMET**, on average, is several hundred thousand miles long.

COMETS HAVE **ELLIPTICAL ORBITS** THAT START FROM THE FAR REACHES OF THE SOLAR SYSTEM, GO AROUND THE SUN, THEN TRAVEL BACK OUT TO WHERE THEY CAME FROM.

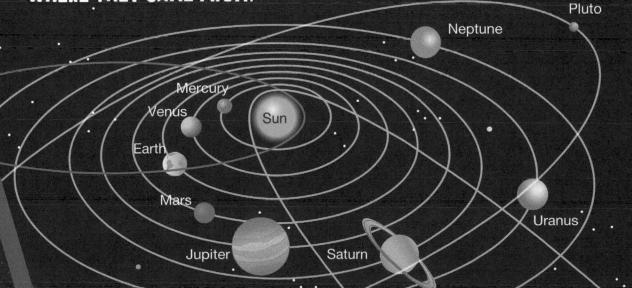

Pluto

Neptune

Mercury

Venus

Sun

Earth

Mars

Uranus

Jupiter

Saturn

HALLEY'S COMET

In 1705, Edmond Halley was the first to predict that comets had **REPETITIVE ORBITS** around the Sun, rather than a single pass.

Although he died in 1742, Edmond Halley's prediction of a returning comet came true on Christmas night, 1758. The comet he was studying was named **HALLEY'S COMET** after him.

THE **NUCLEUS**, OR CORE, OF HALLEY'S COMET IS ABOUT 9 MILES ACROSS.

Halley's Comet has an ORBIT of 75 years. It was last visible in 1986 and won't return until 2061.

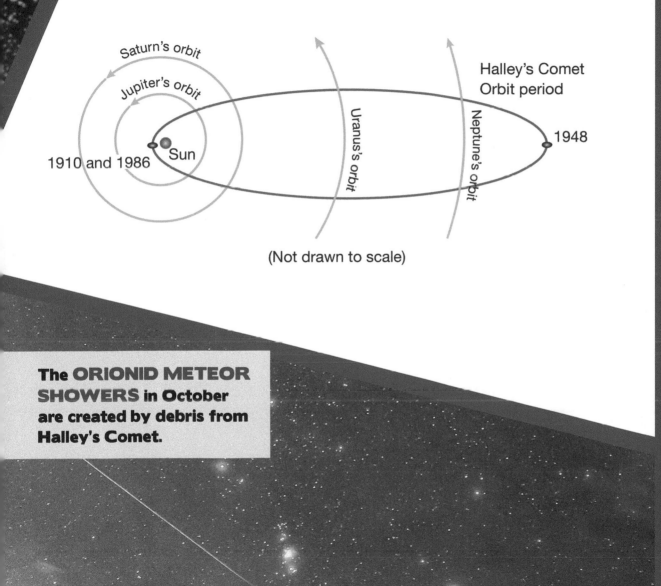

Saturn's orbit

Jupiter's orbit

Halley's Comet Orbit period

Sun

1910 and 1986

Uranus's orbit

Neptune's orbit

1948

(Not drawn to scale)

The ORIONID METEOR SHOWERS in October are created by debris from Halley's Comet.

COMET HALE-BOPP

COMET HALE-BOPP is named after two amateur astronomers, Alan Hale and Thomas Bopp, who discovered it simultaneously in separate locations.

Comet Hale–Bopp is unusually bright because of its large size. Astronomers estimate its **NUCLEUS** to be some 25 miles across.

HALE–BOPP REMAINED VISIBLE TO THE NAKED EYE FOR 18 MONTHS FROM 1996 TO 1997, STILL A RECORD TO THIS DAY!

Comet Hale–Bopp is known as a **LONG-PERIOD COMET**. Last visible in 1997, it's not expected to return for about 2,500 years—its orbit is *that* long!

SHOEMAKER-LEVY 9

In 1993, Eugene and Carolyn Shoemaker and David Levy discovered the comet **SHOEMAKER-LEVY 9**, their ninth comet discovery together.

Shoemaker–Levy 9 collided with Jupiter in July 1994!

JUPITER'S GRAVITY caused Shoemaker–Levy 9 to break into more than 20 pieces before it ever collided with the planet.

Over a period of six days on Jupiter, Shoemaker–Levy 9 fragments created **CLOUD PLUMES** almost 2,000 miles high, heated the atmosphere, and left scars that could be seen for months afterward.

Prior to breaking apart, Shoemaker–Levy 9 was about **ONE MILE** in diameter.

143

WHERE DO COMETS COME FROM?

Beyond the orbit of Neptune exists a second, inflated belt of icy objects called the **KUIPER BELT**, which is shaped like a doughnut or an inner tube.

SHORT-PERIOD COMETS, WHICH HAVE AN ORBIT OF FEWER THAN 200 YEARS, ARE THOUGHT TO COME FROM THE KUIPER BELT.

The Kuiper Belt is named after GERARD KUIPER, who was the first astronomer to predict its existence.

The *Pioneer 10* was the first spacecraft to enter the Kuiper Belt in 1983.

PLUTO was the first Kuiper Belt Object (KBO) discovered and is called King of the Kuiper Belt because it is the largest KBO.

More than 2,000 objects have been documented from the Kuiper Belt, but astronomers believe there are hundreds of thousands more.

THE OORT CLOUD

Long-period comets, with orbits longer than 200 years, are thought to come from the **OORT CLOUD**. The Oort cloud is named after Jan Oort, who first hypothesized its existence.

THE EXISTENCE OF THE OORT CLOUD HAS YET TO BE PROVEN. IT'S BELIEVED TO BE A SPHERE SHAPE SURROUNDING OUR SOLAR SYSTEM THAT CONTAINS TRILLIONS OF ICY OBJECTS.

The *Voyager 1* and *2*, which have left the
heliosphere, will eventually arrive at the
Oort cloud, but not for about 300 years.

Chapter 5

OUTER SPACE

THERE ARE ABOUT 2 TRILLION GALAXIES IN OUR UNIVERSE. SOME ARE ELLIPTICAL, OR OVAL-SHAPED. SOME, LIKE THE MILKY WAY, ARE SPIRAL-SHAPED AND LOOK LIKE PINWHEELS. OTHERS ARE IRREGULAR, HAVING NO REAL SHAPE.

BETWEEN THE STARS

WHEN YOU SEE THE MILKY WAY GALAXY ACROSS THE NIGHT SKY, 15 PERCENT OF WHAT YOU ARE SEEING IS INTERSTELLAR MEDIUM.

Interstellar medium is all the "STUFF" found between stars.

Interstellar medium is 99 percent hydrogen and helium gas and 1 percent dust.

150

DUST between stars can block, reflect, or dim the light given off by the stars.

WELCOME TO THE
MILKY WAY GALAXY

The Milky Way is a **SPIRAL GALAXY**, meaning it has arms spiraling from its center. If you could look at it from the side, it would appear mostly flat with a bulge in the middle.

The **MILKY WAY GALAXY** is 100,000 light-years or about 5.8 trillion miles across.

A GALAXY is much larger than a **NEBULA**. The Milky Way, for instance, contains thousands of nebulae.

IN GREEK MYTHOLOGY, HERA SPILLED MILK ACROSS THE HEAVENS. THIS IS WHERE THE NAME *MILKY WAY* CAME FROM.

Our Sun is located about 26,000 light-years from the center of our galaxy.

Neither the Milky Way galaxy nor the Milky Way candy bar is named after the other. The candy bar is named after a malted milk drink that was popular at the time in 1923.

The Milky Way is also referred to as *Linnunrata* or "path of the birds" (Finnish), *Hard Goghi Chanaparh* or "straw thief's way" (Armenian), *Kumova Slama* or "godfather's straw" (Croatian), and *Compostela* or "the field of stars" (Spanish).

EXOPLANETS

AN **EXOPLANET** IS A PLANET THAT ORBITS AROUND ANOTHER STAR BESIDES OUR SUN.

There are more **PLANETS** than **STARS** in the Milky Way galaxy.

Astronomers estimate there may be as many as **6 BILLION** Earth-sized planets in our galaxy.

The first exoplaets were found in the 1990s. Since then, scientists have found more than 4,000.

The closest exoplanet to Earth is **PROXIMA CENTAURI B** about four light-years away. It orbits Proxima Centauri, the closest star to our Sun.

THE SEARCH FOR ANOTHER EARTH

To look for a planet, astronomers can look for a dip in the amount of light coming from a star. This dip indicates whether a planet is passing in front of that star.

Astronomers are looking for planets in the **HABITABLE ZONE** of stars—that is, the zone in which temperatures are just right to allow for liquid water.

From 2009 to 2013, the **KEPLER SPACE TELESCOPE** orbited the Sun in search for exoplanets.

In 2018, **NASA** launched **TESS**: Transiting Exoplanet Survey Satellite to search for exoplanets.

OUR GALACTIC NEIGHBORHOOD

At 2.5 million light-years away, **ANDROMEDA** is the Milky Way's closest major neighboring galaxy.

At 220,000 light-years wide, the Andromeda galaxy is more than **TWICE AS WIDE** as the Milky Way.

The Milky Way and Andromeda galaxies are SPIRALING toward each other at a rate of 250,000 miles per hour. They will collide in about 4 billion years.

There are 54 galaxies in what's called the LOCAL GROUP of galaxies, to which the Milky Way belongs. The Andromeda galaxy, Large Magellanic Cloud, and Small Magellanic Cloud are also part of this group.

159

DWARF GALAXIES

A **DWARF GALAXY** is exactly what it sounds like—a small galaxy. Dwarf galaxies have only a few billion stars and are a fraction of the size of our Milky Way galaxy.

The Small Magellanic Cloud (SMC) and Large Magellanic Cloud (LMC) are dwarf galaxies that are visible in our sky.

Portuguese explorer **FERDINAND MAGELLAN** was the first to bring news of the SMC and LMC to the western world, and so the two galaxies are named in his honor.

Both the SMC and LMC are visible in the **SOUTHERN HEMISPHERE**, which is why they were visible to Magellan and his crew on their voyage to circumnavigate the globe.

THE FATHER OF MODERN ASTRONOMY

American astronomer **EDWIN HUBBLE** studied galaxies and our universe. In 1924, he proved there were other galaxies in our universe. In 1929, he proved that the universe was expanding.

Edwin Hubble was the first to measure the **DISTANCE** to the Andromeda galaxy in 1924. This measurement made it clear that Andromeda was not part of the Milky Way, but rather a separate galaxy.

During Hubble's lifetime, astronomers were not eligible to win a Nobel Prize in physics. That rule has since changed, but the Nobel Prize cannot be awarded after death.

An asteroid, a Moon crater, and a telescope are named after Edwin Hubble.

THE HUBBLE TELESCOPE

The **HUBBLE SPACE TELESCOPE** was launched in April 1990, 101 years after Hubble's birth. It was the first telescope launched to orbit Earth.

Orbiting at a height of 340 miles above Earth's surface, Hubble orbits Earth once every 95 minutes, or about 15 orbits per day. It's moving at 17,000 miles per hour!

The Hubble Space Telescope is 43.5 feet (13.2 m) long with a diameter of 14 feet (4.3 m). It's about the same size as a **FULL-LENGTH SCHOOL BUS**.

The Hubble Space Telescope does not travel anywhere other than around Earth. Its job is to take pictures of **DISTANT PLACES** in the universe.

Hubble has traveled more than 4 billion miles during its **30** years in orbit.

NASA's October 2021 launch of the **JAMES WEBB TELESCOPE** succeeds Hubble's mission.

Although the Hubble is expected to continue to operate into the **2020s**, its orbit will eventually become unstable. Sometime in the **2030s**, it will be intentionally crashed into Earth's atmosphere, where it will burn up entirely.

THAT'S NOT A COMET!

CHARLES MESSIER was a French astronomer who discovered 40 nebulae and 13 comets.

While searching the incorrect patch of sky for what is now known as Halley's Comet, Messier discovered the CRAB NEBULA.

166

Charles Messier was interested in finding COMETS. His catalogue of nebulae, clusters, and galaxies was born from a list of "not comets."

Messier catalogued a total of 103 objects, now commonly called MESSIER OBJECTS. Following his death, his coworkers followed up on other notes he had made, bringing the total to 110 objects.

STAR CLUSTERS OF THE MILKY WAY

GLOBULAR CLUSTERS are tightly bound groups of stars that are very old and have remained close to one another because of the force of gravity.

There are about 150 globular clusters in the Milky Way galaxy. They are mostly found in the **HALO REGION** surrounding the galactic center.

The **GREAT GLOBULAR CLUSTER** is found in the constellation Hercules. Visible in the summer, it contains stars that are more than 12 billion years old.

An **OPEN CLUSTER** is a group of stars relatively recently born from one cloud of gas and dust.

There are 33 open clusters in Messier's catalogue.

THERE ARE MORE THAN 1,000 OPEN CLUSTERS IN THE MILKY WAY; THEY ARE FOUND ON THE GALACTIC PLANE.

M45, the Pleiades, also referred to as the **SEVEN SISTERS**, is an open cluster of about 200 stars. It's visible to the naked eye in the constellation Taurus.

GET OUT YOUR TELESCOPE!

The **WHIRLPOOL GALAXY, M51**, is located right next to the last star in the handle of the Big Dipper. It's visible with binoculars, but with a telescope you can see details of this spiral galaxy.

THE **VIRGO CLUSTER** IS A CLUSTER OF GALAXIES. OF THESE HUNDREDS OF GALAXIES, 11 ARE MESSIER OBJECTS.

M65 and M66 are both galaxies in the constellation Leo. Together with a third galaxy, they make up the **LEO TRIPLET**.

The **DUMBBELL NEBULA, M27**, was the first planetary nebula Messier discovered. It can be viewed with a telescope in the constellation Vulpecula.

170

One of the brightest galaxies in the sky is **BODE'S GALAXY**, or **M81**. It's a spiral galaxy found in the constellation Ursa Major.

The **RING NEBULA, M57**, a planetary nebula born from a red giant, is in the constellation Lyra. You can see the bright white dwarf star at the center, left over from the red giant's collapse.

The **SWAN NEBULA, M17**, is in the constellation Sagittarius. You can see this one with a pair of binoculars!

The **CIGAR GALAXY, M82**, is found in the constellation Ursa Major. You can see it as a smudge of light with binoculars, but with a small telescope you can see its core.

SOMBRERO GALAXY

The **SOMBRERO GALAXY, M104,** is 29 million light-years away and is found in the cluster of galaxies referred to as the Virgo cluster.

The Sombrero galaxy, with a diameter of 50,000 light-years, is about one-third the size of the Milky Way.

It's not visible with the naked eye, but with an amateur telescope or a pair of binoculars, you can view the Sombrero galaxy most easily during May.

The original television series *THE OUTER LIMITS* from the 1960s included images of the Sombrero galaxy in its credits.

BLACK HOLES

A BLACK HOLE is called a *black* hole because its gravitational pull is so strong, not even light can escape it!

The first picture of a black hole was taken in April 2019 by a team of engineers that included computer scientist **KATIE BOUMAN**. That black hole is at the center of the Virgo A galaxy, or M87.

An average black hole has a mass 3 to 10 times that of our Sun.

SUPERMASSIVE AND STELLAR BLACK HOLES

SUPERMASSIVE BLACK HOLES have millions of times more mass than stellar-sized (star-sized) black holes.

STELLAR-SIZED BLACK HOLES ARE FORMED BY THE COLLAPSE OF A STAR. SCIENTISTS ARE NOT SURE HOW SUPERMASSIVE BLACK HOLES FORM.

Scientists believe that supermassive black holes exist in the **CENTER** of all major galaxies.

The galactic center of the Milky Way contains a supermassive black hole called **SAGITTARIUS A**. Its mass is 4 million times greater than our Sun.

Astronomers estimate that there are between 10 million and 1 billion stellar-sized black holes in our galaxy alone.

177

WORMHOLES

In theory, a **WORMHOLE** would be a passageway between points in space-time that are extremely far away, acting as a shortcut or a tunnel.

THERE IS NO EVIDENCE THAT WORMHOLES ACTUALLY EXIST.

Because of Einstein and Rosen's theory, wormholes are also known as **EINSTEIN–ROSEN BRIDGES**.

DARK MATTER:
WE KNOW WHAT WE DON'T KNOW

We know dark matter does not interact with **LIGHT**—it doesn't create it, it doesn't reflect it, it doesn't absorb it. It's basically invisible.

Scientists don't know what dark matter is made of.

We know dark matter exists because of the way other matter that we *can* see MOVES. Gravitationally, there *must* be something there.

DARK MATTER is believed to make up about 27 percent of our universe.

Dark matter holds galaxies together. Without it, they would spin themselves apart.

Chapter 6

SPACE TRAVEL

IN 1958, PRESIDENT DWIGHT D. EISENHOWER CREATED THE NATIONAL AERONAUTICS AND SPACE ADMINISTRATION: NASA.

THE RACE TO SPACE

The **SPACE RACE** was the name given to the competition between the United States and the Soviet Union to dominate space exploration, which began in 1955.

In 1969, **NEIL ARMSTRONG** was the first person to walk on the surface of the Moon. Some argue that this US victory ended the space race.

In the 1950s, **NASA** voted on whether US space travelers would be called cosmonauts, a term Russia used, or astronauts. **ASTRONAUTS** won.

In 1961, YURI GAGARIN, from the Soviet Union, was the first person to orbit Earth.

The first man-made object to orbit Earth was an artificial satellite, *SPUTNIK*, launched by the Soviet Union in 1957.

On his way to the launchpad, Yuri Gagarin had his vehicle stopped so he could urinate on its back right tire. Russian cosmonauts have continued this tradition.

In 1963, VALENTINA TERESHKOVA became the first woman in space, orbiting Earth 48 times in three days.

185

OH, THE TECHNOLOGY!

Thanks to the space race, we now have **SATELLITE TECHNOLOGY** that gave us cell phone communication, **GPS** navigation, and weather reporting.

NASA has given us ballpoint pens, wireless headsets, and portable computers: all initially designed for use in space.

IMAGING TOOLS, such as CT scans, were initially developed by NASA in the 1960s for the Apollo Moon landings.

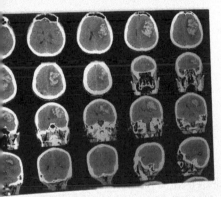

TEMPER FOAM, which you may know as "memory foam," was first developed for use in spaceflight and is now used in helmets, prosthetic limbs, and mattresses.

187

THE INTERNATIONAL SPACE STATION

The **INTERNATIONAL SPACE STATION (ISS)** is a space station that orbits Earth. Humans travel there, live there, and use the station to study space.

The first crew moved into the ISS in November 2000. Ever since, people have lived there continually, with six people there at a time.

188

A TOTAL OF 242 PEOPLE, FROM 19 DIFFERENT COUNTRIES, HAVE VISITED THE ISS.

PEGGY WHITSON holds the record for most time spent living and working on the ISS: 665 days, or about 1 year and 9 months!

The ISS moves at a speed of 5 miles per second (18,000 miles per hour). In a 24-hour period, it orbits Earth 16 times (once every 90 minutes), passing through 16 sunrises and sunsets.

All ISS astronauts are required to speak **RUSSIAN**.

FOOD IN SPACE

In 2019, astronauts baked **COOKIES** on the ISS for the first time. It took two hours because of the lack of gravity.

On the ISS, astronauts eat at a table that is fixed to the floor. Although chairs are not necessary, they can strap themselves in one spot so they don't float away as a result of **MICROGRAVITY**.

In 2015, Italy sent the first espresso machine to the ISS. They call it an **ISS-PRESSO** machine.

The first food eaten in space in 1961 was **BEEF AND LIVER PASTE** squeezed from a tube. Foods are now packaged in airtight containers—and are not in paste form.

SO, YOU WANT TO BE AN
ASTRONAUT?

In early 2020, **NASA** accepted **APPLICATIONS** for the next astronaut class. More than 12,000 people applied.

NASA takes applications for astronauts about every four years. The 2017 class had more than 18,000 applicants; 11 graduated.

You must be between 62 and 75 inches tall to qualify to be an astronaut.

Astronaut **CLAY ANDERSON** applied 15 times before being accepted as an astronaut candidate.

ASTRONAUT TRAINING

After **NASA** astronaut candidates are selected, they undergo two years of **TRAINING** before becoming "full" astronauts.

Even after successful training, astronauts work on Earth far more than they spend time in space. It could be years before they get to blast off!

As part of their training, astronauts are taught SURVIVAL SKILLS in remote places such as the desert, the forest, or afloat in the middle of the sea.

Astronaut candidates must successfully swim the length of a 25-meter pool three times consecutively while wearing their 250-pound flight suit.

One in three astronaut trainees vomit after riding on a plane known as the "VOMIT COMET," which takes drastic plummets to create the feeling of weightlessness.

195

LIFE IN SPACE

Astronauts must **EXERCISE** in space to prevent muscle loss. They have special equipment because nothing has weight!

So they don't bump into anything while they're sleeping, astronauts have to strap themselves into their **SLEEPING BAGS**.

In space, astronauts must **FASTEN THEIR SEATBELT** to the toilet so they don't float away while they're using the bathroom!

Human waste is **VACUUMED** from the toilet and dried so it does not float around in space.

Water cannot "run" while in space, so astronauts must use **WATERLESS SHAMPOO** to wash their hair.

ANIMALS IN SPACE

THIRTY-TWO MONKEYS HAVE BEEN TO SPACE!

NASA trained 40 CHIMPANZEES to fly in space. Ham, a famous chimp, flew in space in 1961 before any human did!

The first animals to orbit the Moon and return to Earth were two RUSSIAN TORTOISES in 1968.

In 1947, scientists used a missile to launch FRUIT FLIES 68 miles (109 km) into the air, making them the first animals in space.

A COCKROACH named Hope was the first animal to give birth while in space. She had 33 baby cockroaches while in space in 2007.

In space, **FISH** and **TADPOLES** swim in loops instead of straight lines. They don't know which way is up!

In 1973, two **GARDEN SPIDERS** were taken into space to see if they would be able to spin webs, and they could!

MOTHS born on Earth are unable to fly when taken into space because of lack of gravity. Moths born in space, however, *can* fly in space.

BELKA AND STRELKA:
PUPS IN SPACE

BELKA and STRELKA were mixed-breed female stray dogs found on the streets of Russia. In 1960, they became the first dogs to orbit Earth on *Sputnik 5.*

The Soviet Space Program also put mice, rats, fruit flies, plants, and a rabbit on *Sputnik 5.*

SPUTNIK 5 orbited Earth 18 times in 25 hours and returned all the animals safely to Earth.

Strelka later gave birth to six pups. One of the pups, PUSHINKA (FLUFFY), was gifted to First Lady Jacqueline Kennedy by Soviet leader Nikita Khrushchev.

You can visit the space capsule of Belka and Strelka at the COSMONAUTICS MEMORIAL MUSEUM in Moscow, Russia.

THE ARTEMIS PROGRAM

The **FIRST WOMAN** will travel to and walk on the Moon on *Artemis III*, scheduled for launch in 2024, the first time humans have stepped foot on the Moon since 1972.

NASA's **ARTEMIS PROGRAM** will begin a series of visits to the Moon beginning with *Artemis I*, scheduled to launch in late 2021.

The first Moon missions in the 1960s were the *Apollo* missions; the next are the *Artemis* missions. In Greek mythology, Artemis is the twin sister of Apollo and the goddess of the Moon.

Artemis III will land at the south pole of the Moon to investigate **FROZEN WATER** found in its craters.

The long-term goal of the *Artemis* program is to develop technologies that will allow us to one day **TRAVEL TO MARS**.

203

LISA REICHLEY lives with her husband and three children in southeastern Pennsylvania. She enjoys teaching middle school science, choreographing musicals, photography, and stargazing. Lisa is an avid Science Fair sponsor who has taken her students as far as the national level.

CPSIA information can be obtained
at www.ICGtesting.com
Printed in the USA
BVHW052109271021
620091BV00004B/4